"What a joy to find such a short book that packs so much in! From cover to cover, there is everything a new leader needs to start thrilling children with Jesus Christ. I will be using this book to train our young leaders, one to one, a chapter at a time. Thank you!"

ED DREW, *Children's Worker, Dundonald Church, UK*

"If you're in children's ministry and you're tired, confused, or discouraged, pick this book up. I found myself highlighting every concise, wisdom-filled, Christ-centred chapter. For those starting out in children's ministry, it's my #1 recommendation."

NICK MCDONALD, *author of Faker*

"This book is easy to read, well written, practical, engaging and inspiring. It's everything I want to say to my teams. The 'prayer pause' takes it from being a book about learning how to do children's ministry to actually doing children's ministry straight away!"

JANE WATKINS, *Head of Children's Work,*
Above Bar Church, Southampton, UK

Starting out in Children's Ministry
© The Good Book Company, 2016

Published by
The Good Book Company
Tel (UK): 0333 123 0880
International: +44 (0) 208 942 0880
Email: info@thegoodbook.co.uk

Websites:
UK: www.thegoodbook.co.uk
North America: www.thegoodbook.com
Australia: www.thegoodbook.com.au
New Zealand: www.thegoodbook.co.nz

Unless indicated, all Scripture references are taken from the HOLY BIBLE,
NEW INTERNATIONAL VERSION. Copyright © 1979, 1984, 2011 by Biblica.
Used by permission.

ISBN: 9781784980153

Printed in the UK

Design by André Parker

CONTENTS

How to get the best out of this book   5

   1. The chapter everyone wants to read first   7

   2. Why children's ministry?   9

   3. Why you?   19

   4. Team talk   25

   5. Digging into the Bible   35

   6. Focus the fun   45

   7. Staying safe   55

   8. The best job in the world!   65

Practice example   71

Further help   77

HOW TO GET THE BEST OUT OF THIS BOOK

ON YOUR OWN

Take your time. If you read a chapter at a time, including the prayer pauses and reflection questions, you'll give yourself the best chance of ensuring that the helpful bits sink in and stay with you—and any unhelpful bits (though I hope there aren't many) float away...

WITH SOMEONE ELSE

You could read a chapter aloud together and chat about it, or each read at home first before you meet up.

IN A GROUP

Read each chapter on your own beforehand, and then use the prayer pauses and reflection questions as the basis for a group discussion.

AS A CHURCH

Download the free team-training material from **www.thegoodbook.co.uk/ startingout**. This will give outlines for a series of team-training sessions based on the material in this book.

THE CHAPTER EVERYONE WANTS TO READ FIRST

IN THIS CHAPTER...

 ■ The secret of effective discipline

THINK ABOUT IT

It has been my privilege to help encourage and train children's leaders for thirty years. Some have been from my own church, but many more have been serving at churches around the UK and beyond. They have come to training events in their area, or have invited me to do something for their own church team.

In all that time, and all those locations, there has been one topic that people want help with more than any other. One subject they worry about the most. One concern that can lead to people not wanting to get involved, or even giving up once they've started.

Yes, people ask for help in teaching the Bible well. Yes, they want ideas for telling Bible stories, running crafts, or praying with children. They want help with children with special needs, or how to lead music when they can't sing. But the one theme that comes up more than any other is discipline—how to keep control of a lively group of children.

● *Why do you think discipline is such a hot topic?*

Discipline is something almost everyone is concerned about—and yet this is the shortest chapter in the book! Why? Because the secret of effective discipline is to build it into *every aspect* of children's work.

- **Discipline is a planning issue:** It's common for children to become disruptive when bored, or when they are expected to sit quietly with nothing to do while the leaders sort out the next activity. Good planning will minimise these moments, and also mean there is an alternative activity available if something goes wrong.

- **Discipline is a team issue:** It is never just the responsibility of the person who is currently at the front of the group speaking or leading an activity. A team that works together can diffuse potential problems before they erupt, and calm them quickly if they do.

- **Discipline is a gospel issue:** Because children who are able to listen to the Bible story quietly, and engage well with the activities that have been designed to support the teaching, are in the best place to hear and respond to the good news about Jesus Christ.

So, instead of a separate chapter on discipline, throughout this book you will find boxes that look like this:

Discipline tip
The "secret" of effective discipline is found in the other seven chapters of this book...

Each box will help show how some forward planning, and effective teamwork, will minimise discipline problems, and help you to handle them if they do occur.

WHY CHILDREN'S MINISTRY?

IN THIS CHAPTER...

- Why we do children's ministry
- Why children's ministry is a fertile gospel opportunity
- We are in partnership with parents, but they are the primary partners

THINK ABOUT IT

When the Kids' Club leaders asked parents what they wanted from the Sunday morning groups, this is what they were told:

> "After an exhausting week, John and I need some peace and quiet on a Sunday. As long as the kids have fun, they'll be happy to go to the group, and we can sit quietly at the back of church."

> "Kids' Club is where my children learn about God and stuff. They do maths and English at school; then come to Kids' Club to learn about religion."

> "I want my son to love Jesus, but I don't know much about the Bible. At Kids' Club he learns things that I don't know yet—and then we both read the Bible story together when he comes home."

> "Carl plays cricket in the summer. But there's nothing in winter, so we bring him to Kids' Club instead."

The children's team wanted to give the parents what they asked for if they could. But were these really the best reasons to keep running Kids' Club?

- *Do you think these are good reasons for children's ministry?*

I heard the gospel for the first time as a child. I will be forever grateful to those leaders who ran the Christian camp I went to, and who faithfully taught me the good news about Jesus. That's one reason I'm so enthusiastic about children's ministry.

But here's what a theology of children's ministry would look like if we just built it on my own personal experience:

- Alison became a Christian at camp—therefore all children must go on a yearly camp or houseparty.

- Alison chose a sailing camp because she wanted to learn to sail—so we must first nurture a child's nautical gifts if we want them to respond to the gospel message.

- Alison became a Christian in the week she first heard the gospel— therefore we can expect all children to do the same.

- Alison used an evangelistic booklet to help her pray a prayer of commitment—therefore we must give all children evangelistic booklets, and tell them that the way to be saved is to pray the prayer in the booklet.

- Alison ended up serving the Lord full time as a children's worker and writer—we can expect that every child who becomes a Christian in our group is destined for full-time Christian work.

Clearly this is nonsense! But it's remarkably easy to base our assumptions about children's ministry on what we ourselves experienced when we were younger, rather than on Scripture. To avoid that trap, we need to look carefully at what the Bible says.

WHAT DOES THE BIBLE SAY ABOUT CHILDREN'S MINISTRY?

Nothing! Or at least it says nothing about children meeting together with others of their same age group and learning about Christianity together. You won't find the typical Sunday School or after-school club anywhere in the Bible. So, if we want to be sure that our children's ministry is Bible-centred and pleasing to God, we need to look at the wider principles and then apply them to our own situation.

WHAT DOES THE BIBLE SAY ABOUT CHILDREN?

A lot! There are clear commands in both the Old and New Testaments about the importance of teaching children the truth about our wonderful God. Here's an example from Psalm 78:

¹*My people, hear my teaching;*

   listen to the words of my mouth.

²*I will open my mouth with a parable;*

   I will utter hidden things, things from of old—

³*things we have heard and known,*

   things our ancestors have told us.

⁴*We will not hide them from their descendants;*

   we will tell the next generation

the praiseworthy deeds of the LORD,

   his power, and the wonders he has done.

⁵*He decreed statutes for Jacob*

   and established the law in Israel,

which he commanded our ancestors

   to teach their children,

⁶*so that the next generation would know them,*

   even the children yet to be born,

   and they in turn would tell their children.

⁷*Then they would put their trust in God*

   and would not forget his deeds

   but would keep his commands.

⁸*They would not be like their ancestors—*

   a stubborn and rebellious generation,

whose hearts were not loyal to God,

   whose spirits were not faithful to him. (Psalm 78 v 1-8)

- ▪ (Circle) any words and phrases that refer to **children** (e.g. "descendants").

- ▪ Draw a rectangle around the words that tell us **what we are to do** for the children.

- ▪ Underline the things we are to **tell** children.

LEARNING ABOUT GOD IN FAMILIES

In this psalm, we see the wonderful truths about God passed down through the generations. Adult believers are to "tell" and "teach" children; who in turn will tell their own children, and so on.

And this isn't just dry information that's being passed on. We are to tell *"the praiseworthy deeds of the Lord, his power, and the wonders he has done"* (v 4)— with the result that *"they would put their trust in God"* (v 7).

But who are the adults who do this "telling" and "teaching"? The language of Psalm 78 is the language of family—"ancestors", "descendants", "next generation", "their children".

This teaching and telling is happening within **families**—something that is even clearer in another Old Testament passage about children…

LEARNING ABOUT GOD EVERY DAY

In Deuteronomy, Moses is preaching to the Israelites just before they enter the land God has promised to give them. Moses reminds them of the laws and commands God has given them to show them how to live as his chosen people. Moses then tells them how to pass these commands on to their children.

> *⁶These commandments that I give you today are to be on your hearts. ⁷Impress them on your children. Talk about them when you sit at home and when you walk along the road, when you lie down and when you get up. ⁸Tie them as symbols on your hands and bind them on your foreheads. ⁹Write them on the door-frames of your houses and on your gates.* (Deuteronomy 6 v 6-9)

It is clear that this teaching and telling is meant to happen during normal, everyday life…

- when you **sit at home**

- when you **walk along the road**

- when you **lie down**

- when you **get up**

… and in people's homes…

- on the **door-frames** of your houses

- on your **gates**

So in the Old Testament we see that adults, especially parents, have the responsibility to teach and tell children *"the praiseworthy deeds of the LORD"*. And this teaching and telling is to happen as part of everyday life.

LEARNING ABOUT GOD IN THE NEW TESTAMENT

This pattern continues in the New Testament—it is still the responsibility of parents to be teaching and telling their children about God. For example:

> *[1]Children, obey your parents in the Lord, for this is right. [2]"Honour your father and mother"—which is the first commandment with a promise—[3]"so that it may go well with you and that you may enjoy long life on the earth."*
>
> *[4]Fathers, do not exasperate your children; instead, bring them up in the training and instruction of the Lord.* (Ephesians 6 v 1-4)

And we see the huge impact of a godly home in 2 Timothy, where it is actually Timothy's mother and grandmother who have been teaching and telling the young Timothy about God:

> *[1]I am reminded of your sincere faith, which first lived in your grandmother Lois and in your mother Eunice and, I am persuaded, now lives in you also.* (2 Timothy 1 v 5)
>
> *[14]But as for you, continue in what you have learned and have become convinced of, because you know those from whom you learned it, [15]and how from infancy you have known the Holy Scriptures, which are able to make you wise for salvation through faith in Christ Jesus.* (2 Timothy 3 v 14-15)

BIBLICAL PRINCIPLES FOR TEACHING CHILDREN

So, what principles can we take from the Bible to help us shape our ministry with children?

- **Adults are to teach and tell children about God.** This teaching is to be continually passed down from one generation to the next.

- Ideally, this is to happen as **part of everyday life**.

- **The primary responsibility for teaching and telling children lies with parents.**

But a typical children's group meets once a week for an hour or so, usually without the parents there, so how does that fit in? Before we answer that, let's have a prayer pause…

PRAYER PAUSE

Think of three children from your group—I suggest choosing a range of children, e.g. a mix of ages, or of Christian background, or of character. If you're not yet involved in a children's group, just choose three children from church that you know. Write their names here:

1.

2.

3.

Throughout this book we will pause every now and then to pray for these same children. As a starting point:

- Thank God that each child comes to the group/church. Don't take this for granted. Thank God for bringing them somewhere where they will learn *"the praiseworthy deeds of the LORD"*.

- Think of one specific thing each child needs to learn or to grow in their understanding of (e.g. how much God loves them, why they can trust God when they are worried or scared, who Jesus is and why he came). Ask God to help each child learn the thing you have thought of this week.

BIBLICAL PRINCIPLES FOR CHILDREN'S MINISTRY

Having prayed for some of the children in your group, let's think how the biblical principles we have found can be applied to how we teach these children.

- The pattern in the Bible is that **adults are to teach and tell children about God**. The things we teach are to include *"the praiseworthy deeds of the LORD, his power, and the wonders he has done"* (Psalm 78 v 4)— and also his *law* (v 5) and *commands* (v 7). So we will tell children about the exciting, wonderful things that God has done, which show what an amazing, wonderful, glorious Lord he is. And we will also teach them the way God wants us to live as his people.

- This teaching is to be **passed down from one generation to the next**. This implies that the adults who do the teaching are already believers (more about that in the next chapter).

- The children's group you are involved with may only meet once a week, but we will also take what opportunities we can to be involved in the **everyday lives** of the children in that group. At the simplest level this means asking them about their lives, being interested in what they do, and praying for them day to day. It may also involve spending time with them during a camp or weekend away; or simply spotting them when you are out shopping and taking the time to stop for a chat.

> **Discipline tip**
> If you have a child who finds it particularly difficult to behave well, ask his or her parents for ideas. They will already know which strategies do or don't help their child to stay focused.

- We are in partnership with the parents of the children in our groups. But since the **primary responsibility for teaching and telling children lies with their parents**, we are the *lesser* partner. So we will do whatever we can to support parents and help them in the spiritual upbringing of their children. Which makes this a good moment for another prayer pause…

PRAYER PAUSE

Do you know the parents of the three children you listed opposite? Whether you do or not, pray the following for them. (But if you don't know the parents, have a think about how you can begin to get to know them some time soon.)

If one or both of a child's parents are Christians, ask God to help them to be teaching and telling their child about him, and to be finding ways to build that into everyday life.

If one or both of the child's parents are not Christians, ask God to use their link with your church to open their eyes to the wonderful truths of the gospel message about Jesus. Ask him to bring these parents to know him for themselves, so they can then be teaching and telling their children about him.

WHY IS CHILDREN'S MINISTRY A FERTILE GOSPEL MINISTRY?

If you know any under-11s well, you'll know how great they are. This is an age of discovery, when they are learning new things all the time. So here are four reasons why children's ministry is fertile ground for the gospel:

- **The good news is just right for everyone.** Think of the range of children in your group, or the wider church family: they will vary according to age, sex, cultural background, academic achievement, and ability at sport or languages or being able to sing in tune or... But for every single child on that list the gospel is *exactly the perfect message* they need to hear. The good news about Jesus is exactly right for every single one of them.

- **Children soak in new things all the time.** They haven't yet become bored with learning. They don't assume they know everything. They haven't closed their minds or put up barriers in the way older teens and adults can do. They are open to new things, ready to listen, and often have a streak of enthusiasm running through them that is eager to find something to be excited about.

- **Children already know that they are sinners** (though this is becoming less true as modern children are increasingly told how wonderful they are!). One huge difference between children and adults is that children have far more experience of being in the wrong! Many of them get told off every day at home or school for doing what they shouldn't or not doing what they should. They're used to making a mess of things. Even the well-behaved ones know how easy it is to mess up, or have the experience of being caught up in a larger group of children who all get punished together. Compare that with what John says in **1 John 1 v 8-9**: *"If we claim to be without sin, we deceive ourselves and the truth is not in us. If we confess our sins, he is faithful and just and will forgive us our sins and purify us from all unrighteousness."* I've met many adults who "claim to be without sin" (or, at least, without enough sin to need saving from it!)—but children find it much easier to recognise their own sinfulness, and therefore see what wonderfully good news it is to be offered forgiveness through Christ.

- **In children's ministry we can build the teaching up over time.** This is in contrast to many adult evangelistic events, which tend to be one-off opportunities that we try and encourage our non-Christians friends to come to. But much of children's ministry is regular (often weekly) and so gives us the time to build and develop a child's understanding of the good news about Jesus.

> **Discipline tip**
> Some of your children will have moved up from a younger group. Ask their previous leaders to let you know about any children who need particular strategies to help them settle, and which children to keep them with (or apart from!).

Discipline tip

Children often know they are sinful—and so do we! How does that help us with discipline? It means we won't be surprised when a child behaves badly. Instead, it's a reminder that we all fall short of God's standards—us as well as the children. Why not use **Romans 3 v 23-24** as a basis for praying for the children (and perhaps especially for any who seem to be particularly prone to bad behaviour)?

- *"All have sinned and fall short of the glory of God"* (v 23)—ask God to help these children recognise that this is true of them.

- *"All are justified freely by his grace through the redemption that came by Christ Jesus"* (v 24)—thank God that the grace he shows us in Jesus is enough to *"justify freely"* anyone—adult or child—who puts their trust in Jesus.

Praying for the children in this way will help change how you feel about them, and strengthen your desire to see them understand and respond to the good news of forgiveness that is offered freely because of Christ.

QUESTIONS FOR REFLECTION

- *Adults are to "teach and tell children about God". This teaching is to be continually passed down from one generation to the next. Who first taught and told you about God (even if you were an adult yourself by then)?*

- *The primary responsibility for the spiritual education of children lies with parents (not with the children's ministry or wider church). What impact does that have on how you see your own role?*

- *We are in partnership with parents. How can you show interest in parents and their families, and be an encouragement to them?*

WHY YOU?

IN THIS CHAPTER...

- The importance of a godly life
- Using your skills and time well
- There's no such thing as "just a helper"

THINK ABOUT IT

When the group had left, Ted thought back over the meeting. He'd asked everyone why they wanted to join the children's team. It was amazing how different their answers were:

Janet: "I've been a teacher for over 40 years. Now that I'm retired, I want to use my skills at church. I've noticed that the children's group gets very noisy sometimes. That's something I'll fix for you—I'm good at discipline."

Marcus: "I'm a great guitarist. They didn't have room for me in the music group, so I reckoned I'd do the music for the kids instead."

Sally: "I haven't been a Christian very long, and don't know my Bible very well. But I do love children, so I thought maybe I could make the juice or something."

Ted thought about the children's group. It definitely needed another team member. But who should he choose?

- *Who should Ted choose to join the team and why?*

Do you have an "ideal children's leader" in your mind? Perhaps they look something like this:

- Brilliant at teaching the Bible in a way that's so engaging that every child is on the edge of their seat listening

- Amazingly creative, able to come up with visual aids or craft activities at a moment's notice

- A great musician, able to play stunning guitar riffs between verses

- Hugely popular with the children

- Has a natural level of authority that means it never even occurs to the children to misbehave

- Able to run around leading exciting, energetic games for hours on end

- Slim, fit, good looking and with excellent teeth

Don't worry if you don't recognise yourself in this list! As we look at the Bible, we'll see that God has far more realistic (as well as more important) things he looks for when he chooses people to serve him.

THE IMPORTANCE OF A GODLY LIFE

As we saw in the last chapter, the Bible doesn't talk about the kind of typical weekly children's ministry many of us are involved in today. Instead we need to look at the wider biblical principles and apply them to our own situation.

The same is true when we think about the right people to join a children's team. There aren't any children's leaders in the Bible. But it has plenty to say about Christian leadership, including some pretty scary lists about the qualities required of them (see, for example, 1 Timothy 3 v 1-12 and Titus 1 v 6-9).

But at its simplest, the requirement for any leader is that they are a genuine Christian, who knows and loves the Lord, and who wants to honour God in the way they live.

For example, when the new, young

> **Discipline tip**
> Paul tells Timothy to "set an example" to others in the church. We need to do the same for the children in our groups. They will watch everyone in the team (not just the overall leader) and copy their example. So a very simple way to help children behave well is for all of the team to be taking part, listening quietly, and staying focused on the activity in hand.

church in the book of Acts needed to add extra people to their leadership team:

They chose Stephen, a man full of faith and of the Holy Spirit. (Acts 6 v 5)

In the same way, when Ted chooses someone new for his team, the top consideration must be that they are genuine, believing Christians, who are showing evidence of that in their lives.

And when Paul was writing to a new young leader called Timothy, he told him:

[12]Don't let anyone look down on you because you are young, but set an example for the believers in speech, in conduct, in love, in faith and in purity. [13]Until I come, devote yourself to the public reading of Scripture, to preaching and to teaching. [14]Do not neglect your gift, which was given you through prophecy when the body of elders laid their hands on you.

[15]Be diligent in these matters; give yourself wholly to them, so that everyone may see your progress. [16]Watch your life and doctrine closely. Persevere in them, because if you do, you will save both yourself and your hearers. (1 Timothy 4 v 12-16)

Timothy had a responsibility to **teach the Bible** faithfully and regularly—but Paul also reminds him of the importance of **how he lives his life**. Paul tells him to *"watch your life* (how you live for God) *and doctrine* (what you teach about God) *closely"* (v 16).

PRAYER PAUSE

Read Paul's instructions to Timothy again, looking especially at the comments about how to live a godly life (verses 12 and 16), but as if they were written to you.

- Is there anything in that list that you need to ask for God's help in?

- Anything you need to ask his forgiveness for?

- Do you recognise any areas where your life has already changed to be more godly? (Ask someone who knows you well, if you're not sure.) Thank God for working these changes in your life.

Pray these things through now.

USING SKILLS AND TIME WELL

All of us have gifts that have been given to us by God so that we can use them to serve him. Some of them are obvious skills that we can easily see the value of in a children's team. But others are less obvious, or more about character than skill. Have a look through these lists to see which of these you think God has given you to serve him with.

- The ability to teach the Bible clearly, tell Bible stories engagingly, or help children see how the Bible message applies to their lives

- Good at music or drama or craft or games or cooking or…

- Good at listening to children

- Knowing your Bible well enough to help children find an answer to a question

- Good at noticing what's happening around you and quietly responding to it

- A pray-er—before, during and after a session

- A peacemaker, able to calm children down (or even fellow team members!)

- An encourager

Hopefully, you are part of a team of leaders, rather than running the children's ministry all on your own. If so, the ideal team will have a mix of different characters (even if there's only two of you).

It's great to have someone who is confident in front of a group of children—but we also need someone who is good at quietly getting alongside them and listening to what they want to tell you. If possible, you want someone who knows the Bible well and can teach it faithfully (though good teaching material can help a lot with this). But you also want someone who is a committed, faithful pray-er, since we can't do anything of eternal value unless God is at work.

> **Discipline tip**
> Effective discipline is always a team issue. If you rely on one team member who has natural authority, you will have difficulties whenever he/she isn't leading an activity. If the team works together—all joining in, and all knowing and keeping the same set of rules—this will minimise discipline problems.

● *What are the gifts you hope to use to serve God in the children's ministry?**

----

* If you find it hard to identify your own gifts, ask another Christian who knows you well. Sometimes others recognise our gifts more easily than we do.

● *When will you set aside time to prepare for the session? (Ideally, set aside a regular slot so that you always have time to prepare properly.)†*

----

† Even if you are not leading anything yourself, you can do some prep that will help you in the session. Read the Bible passage a few times (see page 37 for more on this); then pray for the children and your fellow team members.

Discipline tip

Some discipline problems are caused by being under-prepared. If your equipment isn't working, or the craft materials aren't ready, children will be left with nothing to do while you finish getting prepared. Children often find it hard to wait quietly—a situation that can quickly grow into poor behaviour.

"JUST A HELPER"?

I often hear people tell me that they aren't children's leaders; they're "just a helper". By which they mean that they "just" turn up to be an extra pair of hands in the activities, and to do things like pouring the juice for refreshments.

But I always tell them that "there's no such thing as 'just a helper'!" I have three reasons for this:

1. **Children don't see any difference.** They see all the adults in the room as "leaders"—and also see any teenagers as being "adults". (Young children don't judge age very clearly—I was only twelve the first time a child asked me how many children I had!)

2. **Every team member has the same opportunity to model what it is to be a Bible-loving Christian.** In fact, the most likely time for children to ask questions about Christian things is when involved in a follow-up activity such as craft. So the person who is "just helping" with craft may be more likely to get asked a question than the person who was doing the upfront teaching.

3. **Every member of the team can make a difference**, no matter what their role is within the session. And that's what our next chapter is all about...

QUESTIONS FOR REFLECTION

- *Think about a typical group time with the children. What opportunities do you have to show that you know and love God yourself?*

- *When else do the children see you? (E.g. before and after the group session; other occasions at church; elsewhere, such as out shopping or at the school gate...) Do they see you modelling a godly life at these times?*

- *Imagine the children spend a whole week with you. Would the life they see you living every day fit with the things they hear you teaching during a group time?*

TEAM TALK

IN THIS CHAPTER...

- How to "POP"
- Supporting the rest of the team, including the overall leader

THINK ABOUT IT

Ali was excited about the activity they'd planned for the afternoon. It was an assault course through the woods—climbing over fallen tree trunks, crawling under nets, slithering down a muddy slope—all while wearing blindfolds! She knew the children were going to love it, but first she had to explain the safety rules to them. Ali had worked hard to make the course tricky but safe, so as long as everyone listened carefully it would be fine.

To prevent the children seeing the course in advance, she brought them into the main hut. This was the only building on the camp site, so it was a welcome refuge if the weather turned nasty. The rules were simple: close the windows if it's pouring with rain; no ball games inside the hut; leave it clean and tidy at the end of the weekend.

Ali grouped the children together at one end of the hut. "We've got a great game for you to play this afternoon," she said, "but first you need to listen very carefully to the rules. That way, everyone will stay safe and we'll all have a good time."

"It's a pity I have to shout," thought Ali, as she went through the rules. But it was the only way the children could hear her over the noise being made by the rest of the leaders. Their impromptu game of football at the other end of the hut was very noisy, especially when the ball thudded against the wooden walls. And now Ali was losing the attention of the children…

● *Why was Ali losing the children's attention? How could the rest of the team help her at this point?*

The account at the beginning of this chapter is a true story. I'm the "Ali" it happened to. I was an assistant leader with a local Cub Scout pack when we took them away for a weekend camp. We had around thirty boys on the camp, mostly from a very tough part of inner-city Manchester. They were boisterous, (easily) bored and badly-behaved, and it's no surprise that I lost control of them.

(We also held a "medieval banquet" that finished with a food fight, but that's another story…)

At the time, I was the youngest leader on the team and didn't have the courage to tell my fellow team members to stop playing football. But thirty years later I still remember my frustration. We had a great activity planned out, and it was being spoiled because the boys couldn't hear me explain the safety rules. It definitely shaped my thinking about how to work in teams.

HOW TO BE A GREAT TEAM MEMBER

I'm going to suggest that, whenever you are part of a team but not doing the leading at the front, you **POP!**

- **Participate:** Be looking for ways you can join in

- **Observe:** Observe what's happening around you and respond to it where appropriate

- **Pray:** Ideas for ways to pray during a session, and before and after

> ### Discipline tip
> One reason why I lost control of those Cub Scouts is because the other team leaders broke the rules. Just occasionally there does need to be one rule for children and another for adults (e.g. only an adult leader is allowed to use matches to light a birthday candle). But most rules work best (and help the children to keep them) when they apply to everyone (e.g. when someone is talking, everyone else listens quietly). If every team member keeps the rules, it helps the children to keep them too.

POP: PARTICIPATE

Whenever you are not at the front leading, join in with whatever the group are asked to do. This shows them that the activity is worthwhile; it encourages the person who is at the front; and it helps with discipline!

> **Discipline tip**
> Children are far more likely to join in with an activity (rather than messing about) if they see the whole team joining in as well.

- **Singing:** Sing with them (even if you're tone deaf!), and do the actions if there are any. (Don't worry—young children can't tell whether you're in tune or not!)

- **Games:** Join in when appropriate. In some games, your larger size makes it inappropriate to take part, in which case become an involved spectator (not a gossip on the sidelines!).

- **Craft:** Depending on the age of the children you are with, you may be needed to help them with cutting etc. But if not, and there's enough equipment, then have a go at making the craft item yourself. You can be chatting to the children while you do, and they will enjoy seeing your efforts. If you're not good at craft, this may be a great opportunity to ask the children to help you.

- **Bible reading:** If there are enough Bibles, make sure you follow the passage along with the group. Some children may also need help finding the Bible reference (see box below).

- **Praying:** When the group is asked to pray, join in (e.g. close your eyes or put your hands together, if they are asked to do so). Say an enthusiastic "Amen" at the end. (By the way, "Amen" means "I agree". Explain that it's a way of joining in with someone else's prayer.)

HOW TO FIND A BIBLE REFERENCE

Explain to the children that finding a Bible reference is a bit like driving to visit Granny. First, you go to the Bible book you want, using the contents list to help you (that's like driving to the town Granny lives in, maybe with a Sat Nav/GPS to tell you the way!). Next, you find the right chapter (which is like going to the street Granny lives in). Finally, you look for the verse number (which is like checking the numbers on the house doors so that you go to the right house).

POP: OBSERVE

When I'm at the front, teaching a group of children, I've often had the experience of wishing one of my fellow team members would spot something that needs doing and get on with doing it. But I can't say anything to them because it would distract the children.

I've also had the fantastic experience of spotting that one of my fellow team members is already responding to something that I haven't even noticed yet! For example, I had a co-leader called Ros who used to help with our 5-7s group on a Sunday morning. By the time I had finished talking to parents as they collected their children, Ros had often cleared everything away, done the washing up, and created a display!

HAVE A GO

- *Have a look at the cartoon opposite, which shows a children's group "listening" to a Bible talk. What might this team have observed and then done something about? Jot down as many examples as you can think of.*

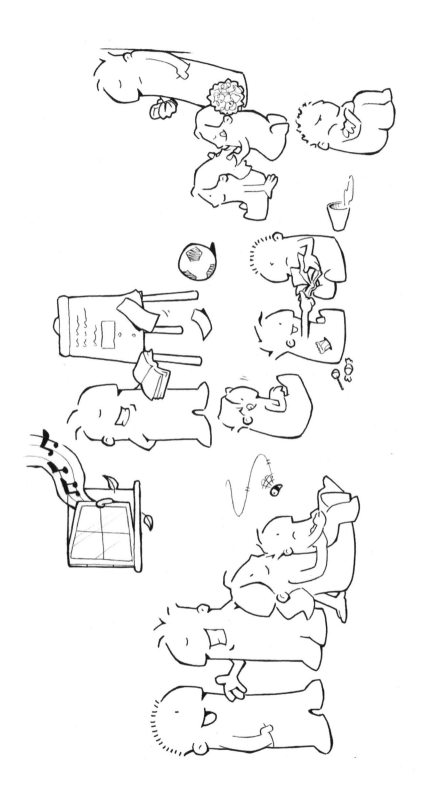

Whenever you are not actively leading something, try to get into the habit of looking around you and *observing* what's happening.

- Is there a problem you can help with?

- Is there a discipline issue that needs calming?

- Is there a group member who needs help?

- Is there some preparation to do for the next activity?

- Is there someone or something you can pray about?

- *Look again at the picture on the previous page. Do these questions help you spot anything else that the team might have done differently?*

> **Discipline tip**
> When you have finished thinking about this picture, check out pages 32-33. These pages give you a further **15 discipline tips** based on this picture.

GOOD PENCILS ARE A GOSPEL ISSUE

A familiar problem in children's groups is the weekly squabble over pencils—either there aren't enough for everyone or most of them are broken. It is well worth investing in good-quality pencils. These are far less likely to break when children press too hard, which means children can get on with the activity in hand (and leaders aren't spending all their time re-sharpening broken pencils). This leaves children and leaders free to focus on the gospel teaching. Good pencils really are a gospel issue!

POP: PRAY

No matter how hard we work before, during or after a session, we will not achieve anything of lasting spiritual value unless the Lord is at work through his Spirit. So prayer is a crucial part of children's ministry. It's also something that everyone can be involved in, no matter what their formal role is in the team.

Pray before the session: For the people leading; for open hearts; for the children to come; for opportunities to show God's love to someone…

Pray during the session: For the person leading; for a new member to feel welcome; for the child whose family are splitting up; for your conversation with a parent afterwards…

Pray after the session: Thank God for the time you've had with the children and the opportunity to teach them from his word, the Bible. Pray about the things you've been learning that day. Pray for the children as they go back to their families. If it's a camp or holiday club, pray that the young people will think about the things they've heard and want to find out more…

PRAYER PAUSE

Choose three children from your group (or any three children you know, if you're not part of a group yet). This can be the same three as on page 14, or different children—whichever you prefer.

1.

2.

3.

Think of something about each child that you can thank God for.

Think of a truth about God that each child needs to learn or be reminded of.

Then thank God for each child, and ask him to show them more about who he is and how much he loves them.

Discipline tips
This picture shows many potential discipline problems, and suggests ways to handle them.

"Lively weather"—especially strong winds, heavy rain or snow—often leads to "lively" children as well! Be prepared to change your session to allow for their need to let off steam.

Loud noise coming through open windows or doors can distract children and make it harder for them to sit quietly.

By chatting to each other, these leaders are showing the children that the talk isn't worth listening to. They are also being a distraction.

For child protection reasons, a leader should not have a child sitting in their lap (see page 56). Gently move the child so that they are sitting beside you instead.

A child will take your lead if an insect comes into the room. If you stay calm, they are much more likely to do the same. Ideally, one (brave!) leader needs to quietly catch the insect and take it out of the room. (Don't kill it—that will also distract the children!)

This group of children is literally all over the place. If you bring them together as a group, with the leaders sitting among them (not round the edges), it will help everyone to concentrate, join in and behave well.

These visual aids are falling off the board (becoming yet another distraction for the children). Ideally, another team member would spot this, and then quietly go up and reattach the visuals.

This leader isn't looking at the children. If you make eye contact as much as possible, it will help them to concentrate on what you are saying, whether you are giving the talk or explaining how to play a game.

This ball is just asking to be kicked! Keep balls, balloons etc. out of the way (and, ideally, out of sight as well).

Phones are a huge distraction for both children and leaders. If you have a "no phones" rule for the children (which I recommend), then the adults in the room shouldn't use them either.

Some girls love to plait or braid each other's hair rather than listen to the talk! Encourage them to sit next to each other instead— maybe with you sitting between them if necessary.

Keep an eye out for children who are on their own and gently bring them back into the group.

If children bring sweets/lollies with them, look after them until the end of the session. This stops them becoming a distraction both for the child who *does* have them, and the child who *doesn't*.

Is anything as sticky as spilled orange juice?! Have a cloth ready nearby to mop up spills as soon as they happen.

These two boys are fighting over who has a Bible. If at all possible, keep enough Bibles in your room for every child to have one. As well as helping avoid fights like these, it shows the children that we see Bible time as important.

TEAM TOGETHER

The *Oxford English Dictionary* definition of "teamwork" is: "combined effort, organised co-operation". Sadly, I can think of a few teams I've been part of that were neither organised nor co-operative! So here are a few ways to support your fellow team members, including the overall leader, so that you work well as a team together.

- **Encourage each other:** Children's work can be hard and tiring at times, so look out for opportunities to encourage your fellow team members.

- **Be reliable:** Be there; be on time; be prepared. It's important that your fellow team members can rely on you. This also shows the group members (and their parents) that the group really matters to you.

- **Team relationships:** Don't be like Euodia and Syntyche! Paul had to write the following to these two ladies: *"I plead with Euodia and I plead with Syntyche to be of the same mind in the Lord"* (Philippians 4 v 2). Support one another. Pray for one another. And, if someone does something that you find difficult or upsetting, always choose to see it in the best possible light. This can help reduce a lot of team tension.

QUESTIONS FOR REFLECTION

- *Do you sometimes find it hard to know what you should be doing during a session? If so, ask a more experienced leader to give you some pointers so that you can "POP" in the most helpful way possible.*

- *"Be there; be on time; be prepared." Which of these do you find hardest? Would your fellow team members describe you as reliable? If not, how can you help yourself to change?*

- *Think about the person you find easiest to relate to on the team—and the person you find hardest. Think of a way to encourage each of them this week.*

DIGGING INTO THE BIBLE

IN THIS CHAPTER...

- Digging into the Bible is for **everyone**, no matter what our role is in the teaching session
- Some simple tools to unpack a Bible passage in 10, 20 or 30 minutes

THINK ABOUT IT

For once, the children were all settled and enjoying their craft. The instructions were easy to follow; there were enough glue sticks to go around; and the girls who often fought over the colours had at least one pink or purple pen each.

Angela was enjoying helping out. Craft was fun, as long as the children weren't squabbling over who had what. But then the questions started...

"How many fish was it, Angela? Was it four or six?"

"What was the little boy called? The one who gave Jesus his packed lunch."

"Why did Jesus make more food than they needed? Wasn't that a waste?"

"I think the boy really had fish sandwiches. Then Jesus pulled the fish out of the sandwich, and made it into a whole fish. Then he made 570 more fishes. Then everyone had a little bit. That's right, isn't it, Angela?"

Angela sighed. Instead of enjoying a happy craft time chatting about the weekend, she was faced with questions she couldn't answer. But she hadn't known what the Bible story was going to be, so it wasn't her fault. Was it?

- *How might Angela help herself so that she's not in this situation again?*

Are you short of time? Most of us are. But that need not stop you digging into a Bible passage. You'll be amazed at how much you can discover in a short time. Even just ten minutes will make a huge difference to how well you understand the Bible.

DIGGING INTO THE BIBLE PASSAGE IS FOR *EVERYONE*

- *Are you doing the upfront Bible teaching?* You need to work hard at understanding the passage first.

- *Are you co-leading a small discussion group?* You need to know the passage well.

- *Are you running a game or craft linked with the teaching?* You need to know and understand the verses you're linking with.

- *Are you giving out the snacks?* You need to be able to chat with the children about what they've been learning.

No matter what your role within the group, you will do it better—and model to group members what it is to be a Bible-loving Christian—if you have read and thought about the Bible passage beforehand.

This chapter includes some simple ways you can do that in 10, 20 or 30 minutes...

These **three steps** (explained in the next few pages) will help you unpack a Bible passage. Each step takes ten minutes—do as many as you have time for.

Step A = 10 minutes
Steps A + B = 20 minutes
Steps A + B + C = 30 minutes

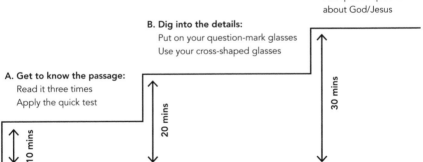

C. Unpack the big idea:
Ask specific questions about God/Jesus

B. Dig into the details:
Put on your question-mark glasses
Use your cross-shaped glasses

A. Get to know the passage:
Read it three times
Apply the quick test

10 mins

20 mins

30 mins

A: GETTING TO KNOW A BIBLE PASSAGE IN 10 MINUTES

Ten minutes isn't very long, but if you use those minutes well, you'll be much better prepared for your time with the children in your group.

Read the passage at least three times

This is especially important if you know the passage well (a particular danger for children's groups, where we often look at very familiar Bible stories). If you think you may be tempted to skim bits, try reading aloud, or from more than one Bible version—or try an audio version (there are several online for free).

Look out for details you may not have realised are in the passage, and check that the "facts" you think you know are correct. For example, in the account of Jesus calming the storm, how many boats are on the water? (Check it out in Mark 4 v 36.)

Apply the "quick test"

This simple test works for the majority of Bible passages.

QUICK TEST

- If the Bible passage or story is about **God**, the main point (the big idea) will be about **God**.

- If the Bible passage or story is about **Jesus**, the main point (the big idea) will be about **Jesus**.

This truly is as simple as it looks. There may be many different truths within a single Bible passage, but there will be *one main one*. This is the big idea that comes out of the passage, and that we want the children to grab hold of. And it will almost always be about **God** or about **Jesus**. And not, therefore, about us, or the environment, or morality, or what we have for supper.

Example—Mark 4 v 35-41

The account of Jesus calming a storm is a particularly well-known Bible story, so it's well worth reading it **at least three times** to be sure of what Mark does (and doesn't!) tell us about it.

When we apply the **quick test**, we see that this story is about **Jesus**—so this means that **the big idea is also about Jesus**.

B: DIGGING INTO THE DETAILS OF A BIBLE PASSAGE IN 20 MINUTES

Spend the first ten minutes on Step A (reading the passage at least three times; then applying the quick test from page 37). Once you're clear on whether the main point is about **God** or **Jesus**, it's time to put your glasses on...

Question-mark-shaped glasses

The best way to start digging deeper into a Bible passage is to ask questions about it.* So imagine you are looking at the passage through a pair of question-mark-shaped glasses, and ask any and every question that comes to mind. There are no wrong questions, though some of the following may give a helpful starting point:

- What happens? (It may help to think of it as a series of scenes in a movie.)

- Who's involved? (Do you know who all these people are?)

- Where does it happen? (Can you find it on a map?)

- When in Bible history does the passage come from? (e.g. Old or New Testament? Before or after the death and resurrection of Jesus?)

- Are there are any words, names or places you, or the children, don't know? (A Bible dictionary may help.)

- Are there any surprises in the story/passage? (These are often a good clue to the main point.)

* The official name for this is "exegesis", but as someone who wears glasses all day, I prefer the idea of question-mark-shaped glasses. It feels simpler.

Discipline tip
One reason children misbehave is because they are bored or confused. Finding one big idea in a Bible passage, and then teaching it clearly and engagingly, will help children to stay focused.

Cross-shaped glasses

If the passage is from the Old Testament, you need to look at it through a second pair of glasses. Reading the Bible through cross-shaped glasses means looking at the Old Testament in the light of the New Testament. In particular, how does the life, death and resurrection of Jesus help us get a fuller understanding of the big idea in the passage?

How these glasses make a difference

You already know (from applying the quick test, page 37) whether the main point of the passage is about **God** or about **Jesus**. Using your "glasses" will help you add detail to this.

Looking at the passage through question-mark-shaped glasses (plus cross-shaped glasses, especially if it's from the Old Testament), will help you dig more deeply into it. The things you notice will help you add detail and colour to a story, or be more able to answer questions during a Bible study.

And if you come across something you don't understand, you'll have time to find out in advance of the session.

Example—Mark 4 v 35-41

Put on your question-mark-shaped glasses:
What happens? (It may help to think of it as a series of scenes in a movie.)

- Scene 1: Jesus has been teaching the crowds by a lake (Mark 4 v 1).

- Scene 2: He tells the disciples to go over to the other side of the lake. They set sail, with Jesus sleeping in the back of the boat.

- Scene 3: A huge storm blows up so that the boat is nearly sinking.

- Scene 4: Jesus is still asleep, so his disciples wake him, saying: *"Don't you care if we drown?"*

- Scene 5: Jesus speaks to the wind and to the waves—and the storms stops instantly.

- Scene 6: Jesus asks his disciples why they are so afraid. They are now terrified of Jesus, and wonder who he can be.

Who's involved?

- Jesus. His twelve disciples. Some people in the other boats.

Where does it happen?

- Lake Galilee (also known as the Sea of Galilee). This is in the north of Israel (see map on page 41).

When in Bible history does the passage come from?

- The New Testament—during Jesus' three years of ministry, before his death and resurrection.

Are there any words, names or places you, or the children, don't know?

- Disciples (v 35)—Jesus' twelve closest followers.

- Squall (v 37)—a sudden, violent, localised storm.

- The stern (v 38)—the back of the boat.

- Rebuked (v 39)—criticised them sharply; told them off.

- Faith (v 40)—trust in Jesus.

Are there any surprises in the story?

- There were other boats there as well (v 36).

- The disciples accused Jesus of not caring about them (v 38).

- The disciples started out terrified of the storm, but ended up terrified by Jesus instead (v 41).

Put on your cross-shaped glasses:
How does the life, death and resurrection of Jesus help us get a fuller understanding of the big idea of this passage?

- Jesus came to be a Rescuer, dying on the cross to save his people from their sin (e.g. Matthew 1 v 21). In this story, Jesus acts as a Rescuer— saving his disciples (and presumably those in the other boats as well, v 36) from the storm.

- The disciples accused Jesus of not caring whether they died (v 38). They didn't know it yet, but he cared so much about them that he came to die for them, to rescue them from something far worse than a storm—he came to save them from sin.

WHICH BIBLE VERSION?

Whether you spend 10, 20 or 30 minutes on your prep, use a good adult translation (such as the New International Version (NIV) or English Standard Version (ESV)) to help you get the most out of the passage.

If you will be using a different youth or children's Bible with your group, read the passage or story in this as well. Look out for words or phrases that are different from your adult version, along with any illustrations or pictures that could help group members understand the passage better.

C: UNPACKING THE BIG IDEA OF A BIBLE PASSAGE IN 30 MINUTES

Spend the first twenty minutes working through Steps A (page 37) and B (page 38). This means you will have:

- read the passage at least three times (maybe using more than one Bible version).

- applied the quick test (page 37) to check whether the big idea is about God or about Jesus.

- looked at the passage through your "question-mark-shaped glasses" to find out as much about it as possible.

- used your "cross-shaped glasses" to think about the passage in the light of the death and resurrection of Jesus.

Use your final ten minutes to think about the "big idea" in more detail so that you can sharpen it up. The quick test has told you whether the big idea is about **God** or about **Jesus**. Now use some of the details you've discovered to develop the big idea a bit more.

For example, **if the big idea is about Jesus**, it might be about who Jesus is, why Jesus came, how Jesus saves us from sin, etc. To find this out, think about the following questions:

- Does Jesus say or do anything that shows us something about him?
- Do God the Father or God the Holy Spirit say or do anything that shows us something about Jesus?
- Does anyone else say or do anything that shows us something about Jesus?

Similarly, **if the big idea is about God**, it might be about the character of God, the power of God, how God keeps his promises, etc. We can ask similar questions to help us unpack this a bit further:

- Does God say or do anything that shows us something about him?
- Does anyone else say or do anything that shows us something about God?

Example—Mark 4 v 35-41
Does Jesus say or do anything that shows us something about him?

- Jesus shows that he has power over the wind and the waves. (Note: Who else has this same power? Only God!)
- Jesus asks the disciples why they are so afraid, and whether they have no faith. (Note: Who should the disciples have had faith in?)

Do God the Father or God the Holy Spirit say or do anything that shows us something about Jesus?

- No—not in this passage.

Does anyone else say or do anything that shows us something about Jesus?

- When the disciples see that Jesus has power over the wind and waves, they ask each other who Jesus is. (Note: The disciples were Jews, who would have known the Old Testament well, so they already knew the answer to their own question! They knew that only one person has this power over nature.)

These answers help us to develop the big idea further. Yes, the big idea is about **Jesus**. Specifically it is about **who Jesus is**.

This Bible story shows us (and the disciples!) that Jesus can do things that only God can do. This is because Jesus IS God!

Step C is the trickiest because it's so easy to forget what we learned in **Step A**!

So we see Jesus' comment about faith (v 40) and assume the main point must be about us needing to have more faith. But that would mean the big idea is about **us**, and not about **Jesus**.

If we keep the big idea focused on Jesus, then we can understand what this passage is telling us about faith. It's not saying we have to have more faith. It's saying that our faith must be in who Jesus is. If the disciples had believed that Jesus was God—and therefore that he had complete control over the wind and waves—they needn't have panicked in the storm. We can trust Jesus completely because he is completely able to save us.

Jesus' question in verse 40 could be rephrased as, "Do you still have no faith in me?"

It's not more faith in general that these frightened fishermen need. It's faith in Jesus Christ, the Son of God.

HOW *NOT* TO USE PRE-PREPARED TEACHING MATERIAL

If you use teaching material someone else has written, whether published in a curriculum or put together by a co-leader, DO NOT read what it says! (Not yet.) Open it long enough only to discover what the Bible passage is; then close it again.

Why? Because, if you read the material straight away, you'll look at the Bible passage through someone else's eyes. And we don't need to do that. If you're a Christian, you have the Holy Spirit living within you, and one of the things the Spirit does is help us to understand the Bible.

So keep the book closed until you've looked at and thought about the passage, even if you only manage the ten-minute version—and ask the Spirit to help you see what the big idea of the passage is.

HAVE A GO

Practise using steps A, B and C on another well-known passage—Jesus feeding the 5000 in **John 6 v 1-15**.

When you have finished, compare your answers with the practice example at the back of this book (page 71).

PRAYER PAUSE

How do you feel about spending some time digging into the Bible passage before each session? Excited to try it out? Or maybe a bit nervous that you'll find it hard, or get the "wrong" answer?

Talk to God about it now. Ask him to help you understand the main point of the Bible teaching so that you can, in turn, help the children in your group understand it too.

QUESTIONS FOR REFLECTION

- *What was the Bible story/passage in your most recent children's session? (Choose a recent sermon if you haven't been in a children's session yet.)*

- *What was the main teaching point? Do you think the children understood it clearly and could see how it applied to their lives?*

- *Were you challenged and/or encouraged by the teaching yourself? Why / why not?*

FOCUS 6 THE FUN

IN THIS CHAPTER...

- How every part of a session can build on and support the main teaching point

THINK ABOUT IT

Jamie came running out as soon as he saw his mum, and thrust everything he was holding at her. There was a crumpled sheet of paper with a scrawled drawing on it; another sheet giving details of the end-of-term party; and a large, sticky model with the paint still wet. It looked like two cardboard tubes, several straws and a blob of cotton wool. Jamie's mum hoped the label she could see hanging from the model might tell her what it was meant to be, but it turned out just to have Jamie's name on it.

"What did you do today, Jamie?" she asked, hoping his answer might give her a clue as to the theme of the session.

"We played a game with balloons. My team won!" he said.

"Anything else?"

"We sang 'Happy Birthday' to Mary, and had some cake. I wanted two pieces, but they said no."

"And what was the story today?"

"Um... we pretended we were sitting in a boat..."

As Jamie dashed off with his friends, his mum sighed. "Which story with a boat?" she wondered. Noah? Jesus calming the storm? Jonah? She really

wanted to help Jamie think more about God, and the things he was learning from the Bible. If only it was a bit easier to find out what those were!

● *How could the children's team help Jamie's mum know what he has been learning (and help Jamie to remember it too)?*

YOU KNOW YOUR GROUP BEST

Do you use published teaching material, e.g. from a teaching manual or a children's ministry website? If so, I hope the material you use helps you teach the Bible well and faithfully. But no matter how good the material is, still **expect to make changes**. I'm the UK editor for the *CLICK* teaching syllabus (see page 77), but even so, every time I've used it, I've changed it!

There's so much that writers of published material, myself included, simply don't know.

- They haven't met the children in your group, or the team who teach them.

- They don't know how long your session lasts (sometimes, you don't get much warning of that either!) or the space you meet in.

- They can't see that your group is full of active boys, or that you have to keep the noise down because the crèche/nursery is next door.

- They don't know if your group is mostly younger ones this year, or an after-school group where the children have little Bible knowledge.

- They don't even know whether you have two children or twenty.

Discipline tip

I once knew a leader who started every session by playing dodgeball—because he worried about losing control of the children unless he tired them out first! Children who've been sitting for a while (e.g. in church before coming to the group) will find it easier to settle if they can let off some steam first. So an active game may be a good choice—but ideally one that links with the main teaching of the session.

All these things make a difference to the session you put together, and how it then goes. There's no such thing as a one-size-fits-all teaching session. You know your group best. *So expect to make changes.*

Unless you have a particularly long session time, there'll probably be more ideas in the material than you can use. So how do you choose between them? The above list may help you to reject some: you can't do baking without a kitchen; relay races can't be run in someone's lounge or with just two children; a Bible history quiz won't work with children who know no Bible stories.

But how do you select from what's left, to give a session that focuses on the big idea in the Bible passage? The answer is to **focus the fun**…

Spot the problem with this session:

- **Opening game:** Dodgeball
- **Song:** Father Abraham
- **Bible story:** Jesus feeding the 5000 (John 6 v 1-15)
- **Quiz:** Recognising different kinds of fish
- **Prayer:** For good weather for the church picnic
- **Craft:** Making paper windmills

We all want children to enjoy a session, and most of them would enjoy this one. A lively game, an action song, a great story, a competitive quiz, prayer for a sunny day, and a fun craft that moves in the wind. Cool!

But…

How many of these tie in with the Bible story? A fish quiz maybe, especially if you add some loaves as well. And perhaps the church picnic.

But if we apply the "quick test" (page 37) to this Bible story, then we know that the big idea (the main teaching point) is about **Jesus**. How many of these activities help the children understand and remember what this miracle shows about who Jesus is, and then apply this to their own lives? *None of them.*

Yes, we want children to have fun—but the key is to **focus the fun**. As far as possible, every activity should be focused on the Bible passage, helping children get to know the story or passage, understand the concepts behind it, and apply it to their own lives. So here's an alternative:

- **Opening game:** Relay race collecting word cards, which the children then put together to discover a memory verse that supports the theme

- **Song:** Anything about Jesus (rather than Abraham!)

- **Bible story:** Feeding the 5000 (thinking about how to tell the story to focus on who Jesus is—not on how generous the boy was in sharing his packed lunch)

- **Quiz:** Based on the Bible story, and maybe other recent stories that point to who Jesus is

- **Prayer:** Thanking Jesus for who he is, and that no problem is too great for him

- **Craft:** A collage of the story that the children can then use to explain it to their parents

If you're working from published material, you apply the same principles. The first priority in selecting activities is choosing the ones that will focus the fun where it needs to be—on the truths God is showing us from his word.

CATERING FOR DIFFERENT LEARNING STYLES

You can read large books about learning styles, or even study it at college, but the basics can be summed up in one phrase:

Different people learn in different ways.

Actually, it's perhaps better to say that different people learn **best** in different ways. So, most of us will learn a bit no matter how something is taught—but we will learn *best* through whichever style suits us the most.

Roughly speaking, there are three learning styles:

- Some people learn best by **listening** (sometimes called *auditory learning*)

- Some people learn best by **looking** (sometimes called *visual learning*)

- Some people learn best by **doing** (sometimes called *kinesthetic learning*)

As leaders, we tend to teach in our own preferred learning style. So an **auditory learner** will include lots of up-front speaking, a **visual learner** uses plenty of visual aids, and a **kinesthetic learner** will plan lots of activities. This suits the children who like to learn the same way we do, but is less helpful for the rest.

So as we put a session together, it's good to **aim for a range of learning styles**—a mix of listening, looking and doing. This will help children who learn in a different way from us—but it has other advantages as well. Children understand and remember more when there is repetition—so it's helpful to teach the same thing more than once, but in a variety of ways. Plus, most children have short attention spans, so it's helpful to change activity (and learning style) regularly.

> **Discipline tip**
> Using a variety of learning styles will help all the children in the group to understand and remember the main teaching. It will also mean a variety of activities, which will help the children to concentrate, and reduce their likelihood of misbehaving.

CRAFT: THE SECRET WEAPON

It's easy to think of craft as a convenient time-filler at the end of a session or to drop it completely if we don't particularly enjoy it ourselves. But craft can be the secret weapon in children's work. Done well, it can include all three learning styles, as well as giving you an ideal time to chat with children.

A good craft activity is never just making something. It's putting something together that helps you understand and remember the story and/or the concept it teaches. You can use the finished item to tell someone else the story (a great way for children to involve parents and siblings in what they've been learning that day). And it will be memorable visually to reinforce what's been learned.

And while all that's going on, every adult in the room (remember, there's no such thing as "just a helper"!) can be chatting with the children—either about that day's teaching, or to build up relationships of care and trust. You can see why I call craft our secret weapon!

> **Discipline tip**
> The beginning and end of craft time can sometimes be moments when children misbehave. Avoid discipline problems at the beginning by making sure all craft materials are laid out and ready to use. Have extra activities up your sleeve for children who finish quickly, so that they have something to move onto at the end (rather than becoming disruptive).

FOCUS THE FUN!

QUIZ TIME

Know the purpose of your quiz e.g. to recap previous teaching, introduce a new theme, find out what children already know...

Set questions at the level of your group. With a wide mix of ages, set some just for younger children.

Make sure that everyone can take part. If you have visitors, include some questions from today's session.

Find creative ways to keep score.

CRAFTY MOMENTS

Use crafts to reinforce Bible teaching and build relationships—not as time fillers!

Encourage children to use their craft to retell the story—in their group and at home.

For younger children, use crafts to reinforce the story. **For older children,** crafts can reinforce the teaching point.

Be thoroughly prepared. All materials ready, and a sample to show.

Crafts always take longer than you expect...

... but you also need something extra planned for the child who finishes in three minutes!

GAME FOR A LAUGH

Choose a variety of games. Different children enjoy different kinds of game.

Be thoroughly prepared. This avoids children waiting around while you get ready.

Explain clearly. With very young children, only give one instruction at a time and wait until they have done it.

Don't let a game run on too long.

Be careful with elimination games. When a child is "out", can they join in again in a different way?

Whenever possible and appropriate, leaders join in with the game.

Make the link between the game and the Bible teaching—spell it out (for younger children) or draw it out (with older children).

REMEMBER REMEMBER

Teach the meaning of a memory verse as well as the words.

Teach the Bible reference to children old enough to look it up.

Check that the verse does support the teaching theme.

Repetition, with variety, helps children understand and remember.

PRAYER PAUSE

Think about any of the children in your group who struggle to stay focused on what you're teaching (and who may end up behaving badly as a result).

- Pray for each child by name, asking God to help them to be excited about what he is showing them in his word this week.

- Ask God to help you, and the others involved in this next session, to plan and lead it in a way that focuses the fun on the big idea of the Bible passage.

Discipline tip

Some games involve choosing one or two children to play a special part (which can lead to squabbles if others think your choice is unfair!). To avoid this, make a "Whose turn?" tin. Take two tins/boxes that held sticking plasters, and stick them back to back with sticky tape. Label one tin "Whose turn?"; the other one "Not mine". Write the children's names onto strips of card; then put them all into the "Whose turn?" side. When you need to choose a child to start a game, pick a card out of the tin. Then put that card into the "Not mine" side. Keep doing this until everyone has had a go (which may take several weeks); then move all the cards back into the "Whose turn?" side of the tin to start again.

BACK TO JAMIE

At the beginning of this chapter, we saw what a struggle it was for Jamie's mum to know which Bible story he had been learning about that day. She wanted to help him think more about the Bible teaching, but she had very little to help her.

If we apply the principles from this chapter to "focus the fun" on the main Bible teaching, it will help Jamie to understand and remember the teaching— and help Jamie's mum as well. For example:

- The craft Jamie takes home will have been designed to help recap the teaching. In fact, an ideal craft makes it easy for a child to tell their parents, and any brothers and sisters, what they've learned that day.

- The label hanging from the craft could have more than just Jamie's name on it. It could include the Bible reference, and either a summary sentence of the main teaching or a memory verse that does the same job.

- The scrawled drawing may be hard to interpret (depending on Jamie's level of skill with a colouring pencil!), but again it could have a Bible passage and/or teaching summary on it as well.

- The invitation to the end-of-term party could include a reminder of the theme for the term (giving Bible passages looked at each week), and maybe invite the children to come to the party dressed up as something linked with the theme.

These are all simple things to do, but will make a big difference at home. We are in partnership with parents (see page 13), so will want to do everything we can to help those parents reinforce the Bible teaching when their child gets home.

And it also means the fun for Jamie keeps going, even after you've waved him goodbye!

"ASK ME" STICKERS

Each week, print "Ask me" stickers for younger children to wear home. These can be based on the theme of the passage: e.g. "Ask me: who does God want me to love more than anyone else?" This will encourage parents to talk to their child about what they've learned, and back up the main teaching from the session. (Thanks to Jane Watkins for this brilliant idea!)

QUESTIONS FOR REFLECTION

- *What is your own preferred learning style (see page 48)? Do you learn best by listening, looking or doing?*

- *Can you think of at least one child in your group who learns best by doing? Or by looking? Or by listening?*

- *Think about the most recent children's session you were in. Can you match the activities to the three main learning styles? Was there a balance of all three, or were any missing?*

STAYING SAFE

IN THIS CHAPTER...

- Child protection
- Leader protection
- Staying safe spiritually

THINK ABOUT IT

For once, the weather was good enough to take the children outside for a game. Mark had planned a scavenger hunt for them with a long list of things to find. He gave each child a copy of the list, and a bag to put their discoveries in. "Off you go," he said. "See how many of these things you can find in half an hour."

As the children ran off, Mark turned to his co-leader, Sue. "It's very hot today. Why don't you go and get the juice ready for when the children come back in. I'll keep an eye on them out here."

Mark wandered around the garden, chatting to the children. He was enjoying making up clues for them if they couldn't easily spot the things they were searching for. After half an hour, he called the children back together. "Bring your bags in with you," he said. "We'll look at what you've found once we've all had a nice, cool drink."

Sue had the drinks ready, and a cookie for everyone as well. She'd poured exactly the right number of drinks, so was surprised when two were left over. "Mark," she said, "are you sure all the children came back in?"

- *What could Mark and Sue have done differently?*

CHILD PROTECTION IN GENERAL

One huge joy of children's ministry is that parents entrust their children to us, often on a weekly or regular basis. We are free to teach their children Bible truths and to help them grow in their own knowledge and love of God. What a privilege!

But it's also a responsibility, and one we mustn't abuse.

Parents need to know they are leaving their children somewhere safe, and with suitable adults to care for them. That way they will be free to relax and listen in church (if it's a Sunday group), while their children are with us.

Children need to know they are safe too. They need to feel welcome and cared for, and for the group to be a place they want to come back to.

At its very simplest, child protection is about **every leader and helper in a group treating every child in an appropriate way**. Here's one example from the child protection policy for a local church:

WHEN WORKING WITH CHILDREN:

- Never be alone with a child in a solitary place, or in a room, or in darkness. If you find yourself alone with a child, move as quickly as possible to where other leaders and children are gathered. This protects both children and leaders from misunderstanding.

- Prolonged physical contact is to be avoided. No one is to be touched in a way which could be considered to be of a provocative nature. Contact may be appropriate when instructing in an activity, participating in a game, administering first aid or when restraining for safety reasons. It is advisable to have another adult present, and the child's permission, as the circumstance allows.

- Avoid kisses and hugs. If a child initiates contact (e.g. sits on your lap or hugs you), gently and sensitively move out of the situation. Do this in a way that does not offend the child.

- Do not permit strangers onto the site.

These simple rules will help you, whatever your role with the children, to care for them appropriately. But child protection issues are wider than just this…

CHILD PROTECTION IN YOUR CHURCH/ ORGANISATION

Your church or organisation should have its own child protection policy. **It's important that you have read this carefully, and that you follow its guidelines.** If you haven't yet been given a copy of this, ask for one as soon as possible.

Before you join the team, the people with overall responsibility for the children's ministry will want to know a bit about you, your background and why you'd like to work with the children. They will ask about your Christian life, and may also ask you to give some references. They will tell you a bit about the children's groups, and also what the expectations are for team members.

All leaders and helpers involved in children's ministry (even if you're "just pouring the drinks") should also fill in a confidential declaration form stating whether or not you've been the subject of criminal or civil proceedings, and whether you have caused harm to any child or put them at risk. There's an example of this kind of form, suitable for use in the UK, on page 60.

This is the requirement of legal best-practice, but is also important for us as Christians because:

- we should respect the law of the land (Titus 3 v 1).

- we should be above reproach (1 Timothy 3 v 7).

- our willingness to be checked is part of our commitment to care for the children.

In addition to these child protection procedures, make sure you are familiar with any **health and safety requirements** (e.g. if you use kitchen equipment while doing cooking with the children), and also what the **emergency procedures** are for the place you meet in (e.g. where are the fire exits, and what is your policy in case of a fire alarm?).

- *Do you have any questions to ask your church/organisation:*

- *about their child protection policy?*

- *about health and safety requirements?*

- *about the emergency procedures?*

A CAUTIONARY TALE

Keeping children safe isn't just about child protection. Many years ago I was part of the team for a children's holiday Bible club (vacation Bible school). Each morning we had a break for a drink and snack. We had over 100 children at the club, so one leader had the "bright" idea of mixing up the orange juice in a large, metal urn. But even with 100 kids, they had overdone the quantities, so they left the remaining orange in the urn ready for the next day. (I'm sure you can guess where this is going—highly acidic juice corroding an old metal urn…)

The next morning, all the children and most of the leaders had juice with their snack. A few minutes later, all the children and most of the leaders started to vomit. It's a morning I will never forget!

I'm sure none of you will make the mistake of mixing acidic juice in an old metal urn, and I suspect that cheap orange juice is far less corrosive than it used to be. But it's a good reminder to be careful about things like allergies. One way that we show our care for the children in our groups is by being careful about what we give them to eat and drink (and also about things such as rubber allergies, if an activity uses balloons).

A helpful organisation in the UK, if you have any questions that your own church/group can't answer, is CCPAS (the Churches' Child Protection Advisory Service). Their website includes a wide range of useful material, along with details of regular training sessions around the country: **www.ccpas.co.uk**

Discipline tip

Very occasionally it may become necessary to physically separate children from each other (e.g. if they start fighting) or to quickly move a child away from harm (e.g. if boiling water is spilled). Do this calmly, and by gently moving their whole body (such as by holding them by the shoulders). Check your church's child protection policy for any specific guidelines about how and when to touch children.

Discipline tip

It can sometimes be helpful to take an individual child to one side to discuss their poor behaviour, and the impact it is having on the other children. But make sure you do this in full sight of at least one other adult, such as a corner of the teaching room. If you need to move a child out of the room so that the other children are not distracted, take them somewhere with at least one other adult present, even if this means a room where another group is meeting. An alternative option might be to take them into a corridor or hallway, but with the door open so that you are both visible from inside the room.

In some cases you may also want to talk to the parents about their child's behaviour. If so, be careful and sensitive about how and when you do it. It's bad enough hearing that your child has been badly behaved, but if it's done in the full hearing of other parents it can be a very humiliating experience!

Confidential Declaration Form

In the UK, guidelines from the Home Office following the Children Act 1989 advise that all voluntary organisations, including churches, take steps to safeguard the children who are in their care. You are therefore asked to make the following declarations.

Because of the nature of the work for which you are applying, this post is exempt from the provision of section 4(ii) of the Rehabilitation of Offenders Act 1974, by virtue of the Rehabilitation of Offenders Act 1974 (exemptions) Orders 1975, and you are therefore not entitled to withhold information about convictions which, for other purposes, are "spent" under the provisions of the Act. In the event of an appointment, any failure to disclose such convictions could result in the withdrawal of approval to work with children in the church.

Do you have any current or spent criminal convictions, cautions, bindovers or cases pending?

Yes   No

Have you ever been held liable by a court under the Rehabilitation of Offenders Act 1974 for a civil wrong, or had an order made against you by a matrimonial or family court?

Yes   No

Has your conduct ever caused, or been likely to harm a child or put a child at risk, or, to your knowledge, has it ever been alleged that your conduct has resulted in any of these things?

Yes   No

Signed _____   Date _____

Referee's Name:

Referee's Address:

Referee's Telephone: Referee's Email:

Your church/organisation may have an equivalent of this form that you need to fill in.

LEADER PROTECTION

A good child protection policy actually protects the leaders as well as the children. Sadly, in today's world, it's not unheard of for people to be wrongly accused of inappropriate behaviour with children. This can be devastating for both the individual and the church or organisation they serve.

It's not enough to be sure that you do not do or say anything you shouldn't. Your innocence needs to be clear to see for all involved.

The simplest way to address this is to make sure that you are never alone with a child. There will be times when you need to talk one to one with a child about something, but make sure you do so in a place where both of you can be seen by at least one other adult. This means staying in a corner of a larger room, rather than going into a small room or closing a door behind you. As long as other leaders can see both you and the child, you will be protected from most misunderstandings that might arise.

Your own child protection policy may include further guidelines for leader protection, so do please check that as well.

> **Discipline tip**
> Very occasionally, a child's behaviour can become so frustrating that you might find yourself wanting to react physically. It is **never** acceptable to hit a child, to push them around violently, or to yell at them. If you do ever find yourself wanting to react physically, move away from the situation and ask another leader to handle it. At a later time, when everyone has calmed down, talk to another leader about how you felt. Agree on an approach to that particular child that will protect you from getting so frustrated with them again.

STAYING SAFE SPIRITUALLY

In chapter 3 we thought about the importance of a godly life (see page 20). It is right and good to ask ourselves searching questions when we start out in children's ministry. But there is another, hidden, risk that appears the longer we stay in the ministry.

One great joy and privilege of children's ministry is that we get to dig into the Bible when teaching it to children—and the Lord also uses this to help us get to know him better. It's brilliant! But...

It is very easy to give so much time to preparing the teaching part of a children's session that we allow this to replace our own time spent in God's

word. So the only Bible passages we study are the ones we will be teaching (which inevitably means there are whole chunks of the Bible we don't read, especially if our work is with the youngest children). And it also means we tend only to think of how to apply the passage to those in our groups, rather than to our own lives.

Before we know it, we can find that our own regular Bible study and prayer have been pushed to one side. This in turn affects our own relationship with God, and we become less excited about knowing and following Jesus (even though this is what we want the children to get excited about).

Alongside this, if the children's group you serve with meets at the same time as the Sunday church service, you can miss out on hearing the Bible taught. This means it is important to make sure that you get to another service, ideally on the same day you are in the children's groups, so that you are regularly being taught from God's word yourself.

So it is worth asking yourself some questions every now and then—and maybe giving a trusted Christian friend the right to ask you them as well.

- *What time have you set aside to regularly read God's word and pray?*

- *How are you ensuring that you are getting to church to hear God's word taught yourself?*

- *What has God been teaching you recently about himself?*

- *What have you been praying about recently, and how has God been answering your prayers?*

- *If you have struggled to answer any of these questions, what will you do to make time alone with God a priority? Is there someone you can talk to about this to help you make wise choices?*

PRAYER PAUSE

Spend some time talking to God about your answers above.

QUESTIONS FOR REFLECTION

- *Have you read the child protection policy for your church/organisation? If not, how and when will you do this?*
- *Have you thought about "leader protection"? Is there anything you need to do differently to protect yourself from any suggestion of inappropriate behaviour?*
- *Parents have entrusted their children into your care—and so has God! How does this make you feel?*

THE BEST JOB IN THE WORLD!

IN THIS CHAPTER...

- Our job and God's job
- Growing as a leader
- Why it's the best job in the world

THINK ABOUT IT

Mitch thought back over 40 years of children's work. He couldn't pretend it had all been easy—at times he was tearing his hair out (what was left of it) over the behaviour of the boys, or the way the girls kept falling out with each other. Sometimes it felt like hard, hard work. And even when things went well, it was difficult to know what difference he was making. Some of the children seemed to really love Jesus, but would that last as they grew up? He hoped so, but knew that teaching children means a lot of seed sowing, often with very little to show for it.

Mitch was looking forward to the service that Sunday evening. There was going to be a baptism, including two young adults. Mitch didn't know either of them, or even recognise their names, but he wanted to be there to offer his support all the same.

When Rowan got up to be baptised, Mitch was puzzled. He'd never met anyone called Rowan, but was sure this young woman looked familiar. She reminded him of a girl who had been in his group when she was nine. Mary had seemed very keen back then, but started to drift away in her teens. She left church, got involved with a rough crowd, and ended up as a single mum living on the estate. He hadn't heard anything about her for years.

As Mitch listened, Rowan shared her story. She talked about growing up in the church, but then deciding it wasn't for her. She'd moved away. But eventually

God had brought a Christian friend back into Rowan's life. As this friend reminded Rowan of the things she learned as a child, God worked a miracle in her heart, and brought her back to know and love him for herself. Now she wanted to be baptised to show the world that Jesus had saved her.

And then she dropped the bombshell. As a teenager she'd chosen a new name for herself. She was now called Rowan—but some people may remember her as Mary.

How wonderful! Mitch rarely knew for certain what happened to the children in his group. He was just one part of their journey, and often didn't see the end. But on that Sunday evening he had an unexpected thrill. Here was someone who'd been in his children's group. Who'd seemed excited about following Jesus, but then fell away. But now was back in Christ, excited again with following the Lord.

Mitch was thrilled to the core. "Truly," he thought, "I have the best job in the world!"

- *Children's ministry has its frustrations, but do you agree with Mitch that it's also the best job in the world?*

Back in chapter 4, I started with a story about a leader called Ali, who was actually me. Now I have another confession to make—Mitch is really me as well (though I changed gender this time, as well as the name!). I've changed all the details and names, but "Rowan/Mary" was in one of my children's groups many years ago, and I did have the incredible thrill of discovering at the end of a baptism service that she had come full circle back to knowing and loving the Lord. It's an evening I'll never forget.

OUR JOB AND GOD'S JOB

The bulk of this book has been designed to help you get started in children's ministry. I've tried to keep it as clear and simple as possible—so that the practicalities of children's work are easy to grasp—but at the same time challenging you to take this ministry seriously and do it as well as you can.

God has entrusted these children into our care, and it is our job to serve him faithfully. So we should be serious about setting time aside so that we can do the work of digging into the Bible passage. We should be careful to plan activities well, and prepare craft materials beforehand, and be sure to arrive in plenty of time. We will also want to give time to praying for the children in our group, asking God to work in each one of their hearts.

All of these things are our job, and it's right and proper that we work hard at them.

But there is a crucial part of children's ministry that is outside of our control. You and I cannot change a child's heart. We cannot open their blind eyes to see the truths of the gospel message. We cannot unstop their deaf ears to hear the good news about Jesus and respond to it.

That's God's job!

And the great news is that God loves the children in our groups far, far more than we ever can. He knows each one intimately, and longs for them to know him too. So we can trust him to be at work in their lives.

It's our job to work hard at serving God well in the children's ministry. But it is God's job to work in each child's heart through his word, which is why we need to be praying for them…

> **Discipline tip**
> We have seen that discipline is a **team issue** (as the whole team work together to handle any behaviour problems that occur), and a **planning issue** (as we put together programmes that make it less likely that children will get bored or confused and want to misbehave). Discipline is also a **gospel issue**. We have the good news about Jesus Christ to share. It's a crucial message that we want all the children to hear. Occasionally that means we will need to remove a disruptive child from a group for a while, so that the rest of the group are not distracted from hearing the gospel message.

PRAYER PAUSE

Think again about the three children you listed on page 14. For each one, pray the following:

- Ask God to work in their hearts, so they are ready to hear and respond to the things he will teach them from his word.

- Ask God to open their blind eyes so that nothing will stop them from seeing the truths about him.

- Ask God to unstop their deaf ears so that they will hear what he wants to say to them in your next session.

- If they don't yet know God for themselves, ask him to bring them to know him personally.

- If they are already Christians, ask God to help them love and follow Jesus in their daily lives.

KEEP GROWING AS A LEADER

Hopefully the ideas in this book will help you as you start out in children's ministry. The principles covered here will apply no matter what your role is in a team or how long you have been serving for—so you may want to flick through the book again occasionally as a quick refresher.

The most important thing you can do to stay fresh as a leader is to keep your own relationship with God going (see page 61-63). We cannot excite the children in our groups about knowing and loving their heavenly Father if we have let our own relationship with him grow stale.

Beyond that, it can be really helpful to read other books about children's ministry and/or meet up with others who are doing the same work. Some suggestions for further reading, and also for training events, can be found in the appendix on page 77.

Discipline tip

Discipline gets easier with experience, and especially as you grow in confidence. If you apply the tips listed throughout this book, they will help you to prevent many discipline issues from ever occurring—and help you know how to respond to the ones that do. And as your confidence grows as a result (even if only a little bit!), that will change your manner with the children, which will make effective discipline a little bit easier still.

THE BEST JOB IN THE WORLD?

I was quite keen to call this book *"The best job in the world"*, but we decided that might not be helpful for people involved in other areas of ministry (some of whom might even think their job is better than ours!). But here are just a few of the reasons why I believe children's ministry comes in at, or near, the top of the pile:

- Children are great!

- Children are open to learning new things (they haven't yet put up the barriers that older teens and adults often do).

- Children find it easy to recognise they are sinners (they're very used to being told they've messed up and getting into trouble!)—and so they really do recognise the gospel message as good news.

- Children love lots of things—games, crafts, stories, drama, singing, cooking, playing, laughing, praying—so children's ministry need never get boring.

- Children love getting to know God, and get excited about following Jesus.

One downside of working with children can be that we only see part of the story of their lives. If they and their family stay involved with our church, we may see them grow into adulthood (if only from a distance), but often we don't. The story I started this chapter with was so precious partly because it's also so rare. In the usual course of things, I wouldn't have known that "Rowan/ Mary" had come back to the Lord until meeting her one day in the new creation.

But here's an encouragement for you:

Some years ago, a dad came to find me and thank me for the children's Bible-reading notes that I had written and that his daughter was using. He was genuinely very grateful for the way his daughter was enjoying getting into the Bible on her own.

I was thrilled, particularly since it is so rare for people to take the time to say thank you for the things I've written. (Writing for children may be the ultimate example of never seeing how God has used your work!) But then this dad said something lovely:

"Alison, one day you will be in the new creation, and a whole long line of people will be queued up waiting to talk to you. Every single one of them will want to say thank you for the books you have written that they read as children."

I was so encouraged by that thought—and hope you find it encouraging too. One day, we will see exactly how God has been at work through us as we

serve him. And we will meet people who, as children, came through one of our groups. We may have felt that what we did in that group was nothing much—but we will see that the Lord has used it to work out his own eternal purposes.

PRAYER PAUSE

Does that thought excite you? Then turn it into prayer, thanking God for calling you to be involved in children's ministry, and asking him to use you for his own good, eternal purposes.

QUESTIONS FOR REFLECTION

- *Think again about "our job" (serving God as faithfully as possible) and "God's job" (working in a child's heart). How does this way of thinking help you as you prepare each week?*
- *Now that you have finished this book, how will you help yourself to keep growing as a leader?*
- *Do you agree that children's ministry is the best job in the world?!*

Discipline tip

God loves to answer our prayers, including the ones we make for any difficult children in our groups. We can pray about our attitude to the children. We can pray for their parents (it can be very easy to criticise parents, rather than support them). And we can pray that God will change each child to be more like Jesus. God loves to answer these prayers, changing both our hearts and the child's.

PRACTICE EXAMPLE— JOHN 6 V 1-15

*Here are some answers to the practice on page 44. To get the best out of this worked example, make sure you have written your **own** answers before you read the answers given here.*

A: GETTING TO KNOW A BIBLE PASSAGE IN 10 MINUTES

Read the passage at least three times

The account of Jesus feeding the 5000 is a particularly well-known Bible story, so it's well worth reading it **at least three times** to be sure of what John does (and doesn't!) tell us about it.

Apply the "quick test"

- If the Bible passage or story is about **God**, the main point (the big idea) will be about **God**.

- If the Bible passage or story is about **Jesus**, the main point (the big idea) will be about **Jesus**.

When we apply the **quick test**, we see that this story is about **Jesus**—so this means that **the big idea is also about Jesus**.

B: DIGGING INTO THE DETAILS OF A BIBLE PASSAGE IN 20 MINUTES

Put on your question-mark-shaped glasses:
What happens? (It may help to think of it as a series of scenes in a movie.)

- Scene 1: Jesus and his disciples sail across the Sea of Galilee to the other side. Large crowds follow him, probably mostly on foot.

- Scene 2: Jesus goes partway up the mountainside with his disciples, and they sit down together.

- Scene 3: When Jesus sees the huge crowd approaching, he tests Philip by asking where they'll get bread for all these people. Philip says they don't have enough money.

- Scene 4: Andrew brings Jesus a boy who has a packed lunch, but Andrew says it's not enough food.

- Scene 5: Jesus tells the disciples to make the people sit down; then Jesus takes the food, prays over it, and distributes it. Everyone has more than enough. Afterwards, the disciples fill twelve baskets with the leftovers.

- Scene 6: When the crowds see Jesus' miracle, they say he is the promised "Prophet" (see below). They want to make him king, but Jesus slips away by himself.

Who's involved?

- Jesus. His twelve disciples. A huge crowd. A boy with a packed lunch.

Where does it happen?

- On a mountainside alongside the Sea of Galilee (also known as Lake Galilee or the Sea of Tiberias). This is in the north of Israel (see map on page 73). Later in John 6, the disciples go *"across the lake"* to Capernaum (v 17), which means this miracle must have happened on the opposite shore to Capernaum.

When in Bible history does the passage come from?

- The New Testament—during Jesus' three years of ministry, before his death and resurrection.

Are there any words, names or places you, or the children, don't know?

- Signs (v 2, 14)—in John's Gospel, Jesus' miracles are seen as "miraculous signs" (e.g. see John 2 v 11). They are called signs because they **point** to who Jesus is (see John 20 v 30-31). There are seven "signs" in John's Gospel—seven miracles that show that Jesus is *"the Messiah, the Son of God"* (John 20 v 30).

- Disciples (v 3)—Jesus' twelve closest followers.

- Jewish Passover Festival (v 4)—every year Jewish people celebrate the Passover with a special meal. It reminds them of the time when God rescued his people from slavery in Egypt. He did this using ten plagues, the last of which was the death of the eldest son in every Egyptian house. However, God had told his people to mark the doorposts of their houses with blood from a pure lamb they had sacrificed. Whenever God saw the blood marking a house, he "passed over" it without harming anyone inside. The lamb had died in place of the eldest son. See Exodus 12.

- Half a year's wages (v 7)—in Greek this is *"two hundred denarii"*. A *denarius* was about a day's wage.

- Five small barley loaves and two small fish (v 9)—as implied, these "loaves" were small, like individual rolls rather than a family loaf. These loaves and fish would have been a suitable packed lunch for one person.

- Five thousand men (v 10)—it is misleading that this story is known as "the feeding of the 5000" because it was really only the **men** who were counted. Matthew fills this in for us: *"The number of those who ate was*

73

about five thousand men, besides women and children" (Matthew 14 v 21). If we guess that each man had one woman and child with him, that would mean Jesus fed a huge crowd of fifteen thousand!

- Gave thanks (v 11)—this means Jesus thanked God the Father, not just the boy or disciples!

- Baskets (v 13)—the Greek word used here was a word for baskets of various sizes that were typically used by Jewish people. Interestingly, when Jesus does a similar miracle in Gentile territory (see Mark 8 v 1-13), the baskets used to collect the leftovers are described using a Greek word for baskets typically used by Gentiles.

- The Prophet (v 14)—the people were waiting for God to keep a promise he had made at the time of Moses (see Deuteronomy 18 v 15, 18). God promised to send a prophet like Moses—someone who would speak for God, and who his people must listen to.

Are there any surprises in the story?

- John makes a point of telling us that *"the Jewish Passover Festival was near"* (v 4). Why has he inserted this into the middle of the story?

- Jesus was "testing" Philip (since he already knew what he was going to do, v 6).

- Jesus created more than enough food—so much that it filled up twelve baskets with leftovers (v 12-13).

- The crowds started out wanting to see another miracle (v 2), but they ended up wondering who Jesus really was (v 14) and wanting to make him their king (v 15).

Put on your cross-shaped glasses:

How does the life, death and resurrection of Jesus help us get a fuller understanding of the big idea of this passage?

- The feeding of the 5000 happened at Passover time (v 4). So did the death and resurrection of Jesus. The "Last Supper", which Jesus ate with his disciples, was actually the Passover meal (John 13 v 1-30).

- The crowds wanted to force Jesus to become their king (v 15), but they had the wrong kind of king in mind. Jesus had indeed come as King, but as the King who would die for them.

C: UNPACKING THE BIG IDEA OF A BIBLE PASSAGE IN 30 MINUTES

Does Jesus say or do anything that shows us something about him?

- Jesus tests Philip to see what he has learned about who Jesus is (and therefore what Jesus can do), but both Philip and Andrew fail the test. Philip says they don't have enough money; Andrew says they don't have enough food. But in the end, *"all had enough to eat"* (v 12). (Note: Why should Philip and Andrew have passed this test? What had they already seen Jesus do, and heard him say? Flick back through John 1 – 5 to find out.)

- Jesus shows that he has power to create food for thousands out of one packed lunch. (Note: Who else has this same power? Only God! The Jewish crowd would have been very familiar with the Old Testament account of God feeding hundreds of thousands of Israelites in the wilderness—see Exodus 16.)

Do God the Father or God the Holy Spirit say or do anything that shows us something about Jesus?

- Not directly in this passage. However, God's promise to the Israelites in Deuteronomy 18 v 15 and 18 is clearly what the crowds are referring to in John 6 v 14. The crowds are correct that Jesus is this promised Prophet (though they don't fully understand what this means, as shown by what they do in the following verse).

Does anyone else say or do anything that shows us something about Jesus?

- The crowds are correct in identifying Jesus as the promised Prophet (see above).

- The crowds are also correct that Jesus is their King, although they are wrong to try and make him their preferred kind of king by force.

These answers help us to develop the big idea further. Yes, the big idea is about **Jesus**. Specifically it is about **who Jesus is**.

This Bible story shows us (and the disciples!) that Jesus can do things that only God can do. This is because Jesus IS God!

The crowds add extra information to the identity of Jesus. He is both the promised Prophet, and long-awaited King.

And there is a final hint in verse 4. This miracle happens at Passover time. Passover is when Jewish people remember how God rescued them from Egypt. In other words, Passover is "rescue season". Jesus was going to

perform an even greater rescue—the greatest ever—at a future Passover time, when he would die and rise again to rescue us from our sin.

So, who is Jesus? He is God. He is the promised Prophet. He is the long-awaited King. And He is the great Rescuer.

Wow!

BY THE WAY...

You'll have spotted that there is a wealth of detail in this story, and masses of Bible links to follow up. If you have time to work through all three steps of digging into the passage, it will help you to add detail as you tell the story, and to answer any questions the children may ask.

However, most of this detail would be too much for very young children. At the youngest level, you can keep the big idea very simple. This miracle shows us that Jesus can do all the same things that God can do. This is because Jesus IS God! For young children, this wonderful truth is plenty to cover.

FURTHER HELP

TEACHING MATERIAL

- **CLICK:** Easy-to-use, Bible-centred teaching material for 3-5s, 5-7s and 8-11s (The Good Book Company)

- **One Day Wonders:** Flexible and fun Bible activity events for children and families (The Good Book Company)

- **Epic Explorers:** The children's edition of *Christianity Explored*. Everything you need to run a four- or five-day Holiday Bible Club or Vacation Bible School for 5-11s (Christianity Explored)

All available from The Good Book Company

HELPFUL RESOURCES

- **Their God is so Big:** A comprehensive guide to teaching young children up to the age of 8 (Matthias Media)

- **Remember Remember:** 100s of ideas for teaching memory verses to children (The Good Book Company)

- **Bible Timelines** and **Bible Maps:** These sets of A2 posters are ideal to help children see when and where Bible events happened (CEP)

- **Dig Deeper:** Practical help in unpacking a Bible passage (IVP)

For more suggestions for resources and training that support Bible-centred children's ministry go to **www.thegoodbook.co.uk/startingout**

TRAINING OPPORTUNITIES

- **Growing Young Disciples:** A series of one-day training events around England for children's and youth leaders (www.thegoodbook.co.uk/growingyoungdisciples)

- **The Bible-Centred Youthwork Conference:** A four-day residential UK conference every January for youth and children's leaders (www.thegoodbook.co.uk/bcyw)

- **Children Desiring God:** National conference for children's ministry leaders (www.childrendesiringgod.org)

- **LifeWay Family Ministry Conference:** For all ages of children's and family ministry (www.kidsministryconference.com)

For more suggestions for resources and training that support Bible-centred children's ministry go to **www.thegoodbook.co.uk/startingout**

CLICK

EASY-TO-USE, BIBLE-CENTRED TEACHING MATERIAL FOR 3-11S

CLICK has a "Biblical Theology" framework, which means it teaches "little stories" as part of the "Big Story" of the Bible.

- Each unit of ten sessions is linked together (often from one book of the Bible).

- These links are reinforced by full-colour teacher's posters and child components, designed to help children engage with the Bible.

- The key teaching points of a unit (this is often the key teaching point of the Bible book the unit is based on) will be reinforced each week, so that children remember and understand it.

CLICK is suitable for church groups, mid-week groups and after-school clubs. CLICK material will help you teach the Bible faithfully and effectively to the children in your group. It is easy to use and covers three age-groups: 3-5s, 5-7s and 8-11s.

WWW.THEGOODBOOK.CO.UK/CLICK

thegoodbook
COMPANY
Opening up the Bible

At The Good Book Company, we are dedicated to helping Christians and local churches grow. We believe that God's growth process always starts with hearing clearly what he has said to us through his timeless word—the Bible.

Ever since we opened our doors in 1991, we have been striving to produce resources that honour God in the way the Bible is used. We have grown to become an international provider of user-friendly resources to the Christian community, with believers of all backgrounds and denominations using our Bible studies, books, evangelistic resources, DVD-based courses and training events.

We want to equip ordinary Christians to live for Christ day by day, and churches to grow in their knowledge of God, their love for one another, and the effectiveness of their outreach.

Call us for a discussion of your needs or visit one of our local websites for more information on the resources and services we provide.

Your friends at The Good Book Company

UK & EUROPE		thegoodbook.co.uk	0333 123 0880
NORTH AMERICA		thegoodbook.com	866 244 2165
AUSTRALIA		thegoodbook.com.au	(02) 6100 4211
NEW ZEALAND		thegoodbook.co.nz	(+64) 3 343 2463

WWW.CHRISTIANITYEXPLORED.ORG
Our partner site is a great place for those exploring the Christian faith, with a clear explanation of the good news, powerful testimonies and answers to difficult questions.